GROW
TOGETHER
SMALL GROUP GUIDE

JEFF MYERS

The Forgotten Story of How
Uniting the Generations
Unleashes Epic
Spiritual
Potential

GROW
TOGETHER
SMALL GROUP GUIDE

Summit Ministries, Manitou Springs, CO 80829
www.summit.org
© 2014 by Summit Ministries
All rights reserved. Published 2014

Printed in the United States of America
First printing 2014

ISBN-10: 0-936163-32-1
ISBN-13: 978-0-936163-32-1

Content Editor: Mike Hamel
Copy Editor: Laura Severn
Designer: Granite Creative, inc

CONTENTS

> Reconciling the generations in the church would breathe new life into a faltering institution and perhaps even save civilization."

INTRODUCTION

WELCOME and THANK YOU for taking time from your busy schedule to participate in The Grow Together Project. These next four weeks together could lead to some significant changes in your life. They could help revitalize your church and spread beyond church walls to influence your city and our very culture.

It's happened before in history.

It desperately needs to happen again.

This isn't a Bible study or typical church group focused on correctly filling in the blanks in a study guide. This experience is about helping one another get a clearer sense of purpose and a deeper connection to those around you, especially those in other generations.

Your fearless leader has had years of specialized training and knows exactly what he or she is doing. NOT TRUE. He or she is a fellow learner who will serve more as a tour guide than as a teacher. This is a journey of self-discovery. What you get out of it will depend in large part on what you put into it.

Look around you. These are your travel companions. Be open to learn from their life experiences, especially from those who are of a different gender or generation, or whose heritage, education and vocation are different from yours. Be willing to share who you are and what God has been teaching you, hard knocks and all.

OUTLINE

Every group is different and will have its own dynamic, but here's a suggested outline to get the most out of your time together.

🌑 GETTING PERSONAL

Each week, have one-fourth of the group give a three- to five-minute bio, sharing whatever they want about themselves. (If these people know you, tell them something they might not suspect about you. Like the time you worked as a nightclub bouncer, or when you sang backup for the Bee Gees. You'll have to tell the younger members who the Bee Gees were. See if you can raise a few eyebrows.)

▶ FILM

Watch a 15-minute clip from the film *Grow Together: A Conversation Starter Film.*

✆ DISCUSSION

Some questions have been provided to prime the pump. They are based on the film and a few chapters from the book *Grow Together.* If you haven't done the reading, bluff your way through the discussion and catch up on the chapters later. What you're after here is not the "right" answers but insights that will change the way you think and live.

❌ REFLECTION

In a college setting, this would be called homework.
Don't worry, it's nothing you have to turn in or that will
be graded. It's just meant to help you prepare for, and get
the most out of, the group discussion.

Notes

These pages are blank. Fill them with pearls
of wisdom and nuggets of truth uncovered
in your study.

Please don't approach the Grow Together Project as
another study to make your way through. Rather, take it
as a rare opportunity to form new relationships that will
enrich your life and empower the church to be all God
has called and equipped her to be.

⟫⟫⟫ READY.
SET.
ENGAGE!

WEEK
one
POSITIVE INFLUENCE?

💜 GETTING PERSONAL

If he is comfortable, have the oldest man in the group share about
himself for three to five minutes. Next, have the youngest person
in the group do the same.

That's a good start. Now ask for three or four more volunteers to
tell their stories; however many it takes to get through one-fourth
of the group.

▶ FILM

Watch Part I of *Grow Together: A Conversation Starter Film;*
"Falling Away" — starts @ 0:00

⊖ DISCUSSION

These questions are based on Act I of the film *Grow Together:
A Conversation Starter Film* and chapters 1 - 3 of the book
Grow Together.

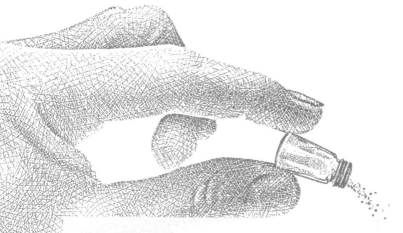

SALTY ENOUGH?

" The church has the same effect on civilization that salt
has on meat; it protects and preserves it. Augustine
said that the citizens of the kingdom of God will be the
best citizens in the kingdom of man. Hospitals. Modern
science. Abolition of slavery. Orphanages. Great works
of art. Free market economics. A rational system
of justice. Care for the poor. You name it, Christians
started it, helped it grow and helped to sustain it."

In each case, the energy of the younger generation combined with the wisdom of the older to bring about change and sustain it. The church was leading in the culture.

Can you point to times when the church changed the course of human history for the better?

For extra credit, do you know if the changes were led by older or younger Christians?

How about instances when the church could have made a difference — but didn't?

✝ CHURCH AND CULTURE

❝ The vision of church as an oasis of transformation for a culture suffering in the desert of vulgarity and starving for meaning has been abandoned — not just by the culture, but also by many in the church itself. Culture is too far gone, we think. The poison of hopelessness runs in our veins, spreading mindless amusement and twisted desire into every extremity until our limbs become listless and numb.❞

Do you believe American culture is headed in the wrong direction — or too far gone already? Give some examples of what makes you think so — or not.

Can you give some current instances where the church is being a positive influence in our culture? Are these efforts being led by younger or older Christians?

When historians look back at the beginning of the 21st century, what will they say about the church? Check which adjectives you think they might use to describe us:

O sectarian
O ecumenical
O divisive
O tolerant
O loving
O judgmental
O compassionate
O marginalized
O irrelevant
O innovative
O insular
O redemptive

Are there other adjectives you would apply to the church?

⊗ REFLECTION

**Come up with a list of adjectives that describe the church as you
have found her to be in your experience.**

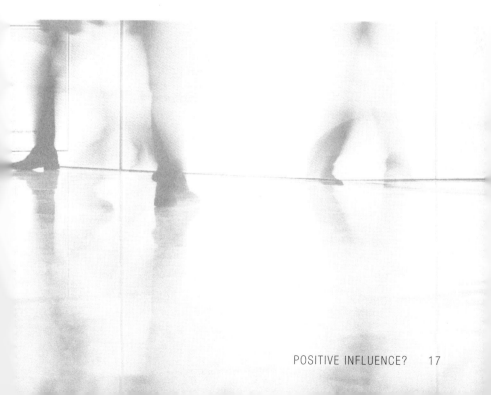

Read chapters 4 - 6 of *Grow Together* to prepare for next week's discussion.

"We do not want, as the newspapers say, a church that will move with the world. We want a church that will move the world. ... It is by that test that history will really judge, of any church, whether it is the real church or no."

G.K. Chesterton

Week One Notes

WEEK
two

THE WHOLE
TRUTH

💙 GETTING PERSONAL

Time for another quarter of the group to share a bit about themselves.
Keep it to between three and five minutes. Alternate from man to
woman and older to younger.

Let anyone who wants to share their list of adjectives describing their
experience with the church.

Ask if anyone has an insight from last week they'd like to share.

▶ FILM

Watch Part 2 of *Grow Together: A Conversation Starter Film;*
"Transformation" — starts @ 13:47

🍏 DISCUSSION

These questions are based on Act II of the film *Grow Together:
A Conversation Starter Film* and chapters 4 - 6 of the book
Grow Together.

TRUTH IN RELATIONSHIP

" Everyday truths such as how to prepare lemongrass
chicken or which freeways to avoid during rush hour
can be passed on en masse. But Capital T Truth —
life-altering, world-changing truth — only takes hold
through relationship. Up to 75 percent of the people
leaving church say they don't feel they belong. It's a
failure of the relationship strand, not the truth strand."

Relationship is the normal pattern in scripture for passing on truth. Joshua had Moses, Timothy had Paul, Isaac had Abraham, Ruth had Naomi, Elisha had Elijah. The Apostle Paul urged that faithful men be equipped to train faithful men, who would in turn be equipped to teach others (2 Timothy 2:2).

Have you had a Paul or Naomi in your life?

If you're a bit older, have you taken on a Timothy or Ruth? If so, briefly share how the relationship came about and what were some of the life-lessons you learned.

⬤GENERATION GAP

" In the workplace, 65 percent of research respondents indicated that generation gaps make it hard to get things done. Many of the problems we thought were related to the loss of employee loyalty and work ethic are actually generational. Generational differences affect the church as well. Just by looking at the characteristics of various generational cohorts we can probably figure out how this is so."

What are some of the differences between these generations?

▶ Traditionalists: born between 1925 and 1945

▶ Baby Boomers: born between 1946 and 1964

▶ Gen Xers: born between 1965 and 1979

▶ Millennials or Gen Yers: born between 1980 and 2001

▶ Gen Zers: born after 2001

Do you have close friends in generations other than yours? If so, how did you cultivate those friendships? If not, why not?

A recent study of young adults who stay involved in church revealed that they do so because of meaningful relationships in which they learn to live thoughtfully, make a meaningful contribution, succeed at work, and connect with Jesus in a real and meaningful way. These are deep identity-shaping activities.

How does your church do when it comes to connecting older adults with younger adults?

One thing that keeps the generations apart is pride.

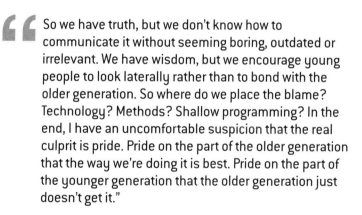

" So we have truth, but we don't know how to communicate it without seeming boring, outdated or irrelevant. We have wisdom, but we encourage young people to look laterally rather than to bond with the older generation. So where do we place the blame? Technology? Methods? Shallow programming? In the end, I have an uncomfortable suspicion that the real culprit is pride. Pride on the part of the older generation that the way we're doing it is best. Pride on the part of the younger generation that the older generation just doesn't get it."

What are some ways your generation — including you — show pridefulness in how you relate to other generations?

⊗ REFLECTION

Review your life and identify any mentors who have had a significant impact on you. Who were they and what did they do that made a difference?

Read chapters 7 and 8 of *Grow Together* to prepare for next week's discussion.

"Make a list of the people who have shaped your life

nd try to figure out why."

—Phillip Yancey

Week Two Notes

WEEK
three

THE POWER
OF PERSONAL
RELATIONSHIPS

♥ GETTING PERSONAL

You know the drill by now; three to five minutes of personal detail
from a few more members of the group.

⊙ DISCUSSION

These questions are based on Act III of the film *Grow Together: A Conversation Starter Film* and chapters 7 and 8 of the book *Grow Together*.

SATISFYING HUNGER

 We all hunger for truth, identity and meaning. Our hunger is satisfied only in the context of multigenerational, personal relationships. Most people find themselves intimidated by this: I have so little to give, they say. But this betrays a manufacturing, not a cultivating, mindset. What we have to give is a matter of quality, not quantity. It's an issue of moments, not minutes."

I'm convinced that the unwillingness to invest in people of any age is rooted in a radical misunderstanding of what relationships are all about. For some of us, life is an assembly line — there's no fun to it, just duty. For others, it's all about comfort — hang around people who make us feel good and ignore everyone else. For still others, it just seems overwhelming to think of having people unload their problems on us and not know what to do, so it is best to just lay low and leave it to the experts.

In order to break through this mindset, keep the following truths in mind:

- O God is not asking me to give what I do not possess.
- O It's okay to start slow and grow.
- O My mess is my message.
- O It's okay to admit that I don't know.

Which of these truths has been the most freeing to you in interpersonal relationships?

Which of these truths do you have the most difficulty believing?

⊙ SELF-DISCLOSURE

> Sociologists Irwin Altman and Dalmas Taylor studied interpersonal disclosure and explained that the best relationships "scaffold" the level of self-disclosure. As you take the lead by being a little vulnerable, others will usually reciprocate. When they do, you can disclose a little more. This builds a foundation of trust and raises both individuals' comfort levels."

Here are four questions that can help you reach the right level of openness and vulnerability in a relationship. Before you share something personal, ask yourself:

▶ Is this level of sharing appropriate for this stage of the relationship?

▶ Does the way I am sharing my past glorify sin?

▶ What are my motives for sharing this information in this way?

▶ Am I burdening others with information they shouldn't have to shoulder?

As a group, see if you can come up with practical benchmarks for applying these questions to relationships. How can you tell if something you might share:

is inappropriate?
glorifies sin?
creates a burden for others?

> At the end of the day, we need a new way of thinking — to change our reflex reliance on programming and organization. To embrace the messiness. To live life together in a way that creates trust and a space for showing how to live godly values in relationships, at school, at work (and in the church)."

Are you willing to share yourself — messiness and all — in a mentoring relationship?

If not, why not?

⊗ REFLECTION

If you're not currently in a mentoring relationship, think about what scares you the most about entering into one.

Read chapters 9 and 10 of *Grow Together* to prepare for next week's discussion.

—Steven

"The delicate balance of mentoring someone is not creating them in your own image, but giving them the opportunity to create themselves."

—Steven Spielberg

Week Three Notes

WEEK
four

LIFE
ON
LIFE

 GETTING PERSONAL

The last of the personal sound bites from all those who haven't yet shared about themselves.

Have all who are willing share some of their fears about getting involved in a mentoring relationship.

Ask if anyone has an insight from last week they'd like to share.

▶ **FILM**

🍃 DISCUSSION

These questions are based on Act III of the film *Grow Together: A Conversation Starter Film* and chapters 9 and 10 of the book *Grow Together*.

COME TOGETHER

" Imagine if the church claimed this idea of life-on-life mentoring as she did small groups 30 years ago. Imagine a day when it is natural for generations to worship together, for older adults to invest intentionally in the younger ones, whether in Bible study, having honorable relationships or succeeding in life."

"The body of Christ is not broken up by generations. This generation should go over here and do this thing and this generation should go over there and do that. It's the body of Christ; brothers and sisters regardless of age, race (or) gender. I think if you saw the younger generations and the older generations come together in a truly unified way, living out scripture … you would see revival, you would see change locally, nationally and globally."
—Jon Bell

What are some church programs where you think it makes sense to divide up by age?

Are there some areas where you believe the congregation should be more blended?

What could be done outside the church building to encourage multigenerational relationships?

▶ MENTOR COACH

 The church is the most natural place for (mentoring) to happen. What is a church but a family of families reclaiming the ancient art of spiritual formation through life-on-life mentoring? It's not about more and faster — it's about deep and quality. We all have a need to be affirmed and inspired and formed and directed. If the church doesn't do it, the rising generation will find someone to follow."

One of the most powerful forms of mentoring is coaching.
Have you had any experiences with coaches in your life?

Were those experiences positive or negative?

What made the experience positive?

What made the experience negative?

Coaches do three things differently from most conversation partners: They listen actively. They ask open-ended and broad questions and give others time to think. They help others set worthy goals. They aren't satisfied when a conversation ends without a clear sense of direction.

What are some practical ways to bring coaching into the church?

● WRAP IT UP

Since this is the final group session, ask people to share lessons they've learned and practical steps they plan to take as a result of the study. Set the example by going first.

Encourage people to stay in touch. Share phone numbers and email addresses. Thank everyone for their time and commitment.

● REFLECTION

Are you involved in a mentoring or coaching relationship?

If so, how can you use what you've learned in this study to improve the relationship?

If you are not involved in a mentoring or coaching relationship, would you like to be?

What steps can you take to make this desire a reality?

If you are serious, make yourself accountable to someone in the group to follow through.

— John W

"A coach is someone who can give correction without causing resentment."

-John Wooden

Week Four Notes

leader's
GUIDE

THANK YOU!

Thank you for stepping up and taking responsibility to lead this discussion group. It will be duly noted on your heavenly resume.

DESCRIPTION

Help people open up in ways that *promote a clearer sense of purpose* in their lives and *a deeper connection to others,* especially those in other generations.

SMALL GROUP LEADER

Being a small group leader can be a rewarding experience, but it will take some work on your part to make the group a success. By success we *mean moving people along in their spiritual journey.* Not everyone is at the same place or moves at the same pace, but you can help one another understand and apply life-changing truths.

◉ MENTORING

In this case, the truth you will be exploring is *how multigenerational mentoring can enrich individuals and empower the church.* Your guidebook for this trip of discovery is *Grow Together* by Dr. Jeff Myers of Summit Ministries. Encourage your people to buy the book and read the appropriate chapters in advance.

Dr. Myers is also the host of a one-hour documentary called *Grow Together: A Conversation Starter.* Each week you will watch a portion of the film featuring some leading Christian thinkers and church leaders. Their insights will inform and inspire.

▶ THE FILM AND BOOK

Review the film clip that you will show; *read the chapters* in the book that will be covered. Check out the supplemental questions and additional quotes from *Grow Together* in this guide. Mark any sections you think it might be helpful to bring up, but don't shoehorn in every comment.

◉ DISCUSSION

Think of yourself *more as a facilitator than a fearless leader.* Instigate discussion, don't control it. Encourage the group to talk among themselves and not to direct everything at you. Try to draw out the more quiet members, but don't put anyone on the spot. At the same time, don't let the more vocal members dominate the discussion.

Keep things moving but don't worry about getting to all the questions. Let the group spend as much time as it needs to on each issue without getting bogged down.

The questions provided in this study guide are based on the book and film. They are meant *to stimulate discussion, not restrict it.* Encourage group members to ask questions of their own and to learn from one another.

This isn't a Bible study, but don't be afraid to bring up relevant biblical passages. Mentoring goes on from Genesis to Revelation. Learning-by-doing is a concept promoted from Proverbs to the Gospels.

❯ GET CONNECTED

This is a short study — only four weeks — but it can make a lifetime of difference to those who **get connected to others** because of it. Pray, promote and prepare with that goal in mind.

Before you start

- ○ Ask the Lord to draw together the people he wants to be in the group.

- ○ Personally invite those you would like to join you. Don't just leave it to a Sunday announcement or blurb in the bulletin.

- ○ Recruit people of different ages, backgrounds, life experiences and spiritual maturity.

- ○ Secure a host home. Make sure people know how to get there and when the group starts.

- ○ Have a DVD player and a TV large enough for everyone to see the film. Have the clip for the week cued up in advance.

- ○ Make arrangements for childcare if you are inviting couples.

A SAFE ENVIRONMENT

 You never get a second chance
to make a good first impression."
—Will Rogers

The first meeting can be intimidating so do
everything to put people at ease. Create a
welcoming environment. Allow for social time
for people to get acquainted or caught up.

Have simple refreshments available when
people arrive. Food helps folks relax and sets a
casual mood for the group. Have a refreshment
sign-up list to share the blessing of serving.

Have some icebreakers ready to help people
transition from the stress of their day to a
relaxed conversation about spiritual matters.
Don't be afraid to get a little silly.

State early and often that the group will be a
safe place for everyone, which means accepting
each other as you are. Confidentiality is crucial.
What's said in the group stays in the group.

◉ SEVEN KEYS

1. BE PREPARED
Don't just scan the material, read the book, watch the film clip and review the questions for the week, including the supplemental questions. People are giving you the gift of their time; give them a good return on their investment.

2. BE COMMITTED
Make the group a top priority for the next four weeks. Ask everyone in the group to make a similar commitment.

3. BE ENTHUSIASTIC
As the leader, you set the tone for the group. Think of yourself as a thermostat, not a thermometer. Be upbeat. Smile. Greet people warmly when they arrive and send them off with a sense of expectation and excitement for what's ahead.

4. BE FLEXIBLE
Prepare a lesson plan, but be sensitive to what's going on in people's lives. Take extra time to share and pray for one another when needed. Dig deeper into a question if the group is interested, and don't worry about covering all the material.

5. BE YOURSELF
This means being open and honest about your own life: struggles, successes, mistakes, milestones. The more authentic you are, the more likely others are to open up. But be careful not to disclose too much too soon. You don't want to intimidate people or put a damper on healthy interaction.

6. BE A GOOD LISTENER
Focus on what others are saying rather than thinking ahead to the next question. Use nonverbal cues to show you're listening: Face the speaker, make eye contact, nod occasionally. These little things can make a person feel listened to and appreciated.

7. BE IN CONTROL
Encourage participation but don't allow anyone to dominate the discussion. Talk to anyone who's sharing too much — away from the group is best. Affirm their positive contribution, then ask them to hold back for the sake of drawing out others.

❗ DOS ...

Whether you've been leading groups for years or are just starting, here are a few timeless dos and don'ts to keep in mind.

DO pray for your people; ask God to use your time together to move them forward in their walk with him.

DO lead by example. People learn more from what you do than what you say.

DO honor everyone's time commitment by starting and ending on time.

DO encourage everyone to participate at their own pace. Draw people in without putting them on the spot or making them feel uncomfortable. DISCUSSION PROMPTERS:

- ○ How about somebody who hasn't spoken yet?
- ○ Anyone else want to add to what she's said?
- ○ Does anyone have a different perspective on this?

DO arrange seating so everyone can see the DVD clip, then circle up for the discussion so there's no back row.

DO make time to get to know those in your group. The relationships you establish are more important than the study.

DO ask people to silence their phones.

... AND DON'TS

▶ **DON'T** make yourself the center of attention. Set a good example by being open and candid, but resist the temptation to share everything you know or to have the final word.

▶ **DON'T** assume everyone has studied the material and came prepared. You're not after the "official" answers but true insights, especially those that come from life experience.

▶ **DON'T** teach — facilitate. Apply the 70/30 principle: They do 70 percent of the talking; you do 30 percent or less.

▶ **DON'T** be afraid of silence or rush to fill dead air. People need time to think. Open space allows those who aren't spontaneous but who have keen insights to participate.

▶ **DON'T** rush people out the door. Encourage loitering after the discussion is over; it's a great time to build relationships.

▶ **DON'T** limit interaction to the group discussion. Encourage everyone to find ways to stay in touch throughout the week: Text a quick encouragement, have coffee, do lunch, chat after church. ... Be creative!

▶ **DON'T** expect everyone to be there every week or make them feel guilty if they miss a study. Life is busy. Give them a quick recap during the week or when they return.

? WHAT IF ...

... no one shows up?

Personal invitations with an RSVP can help avoid this situation. Call or email people in advance of the first meeting. Encourage them to invite friends.

... someone asks a question you can't answer?

Remember, you're the moderator, not the Oracle of All Wisdom. See if anyone else has some insight. Encourage the group to dig deeper. Do some research and come back next week with any helpful information you find.

... there are people in the group who are more spiritually mature and experienced than you?

That's great! Don't be intimidated; count your blessings. You are all there to learn from each other. Tap into the rich wisdom of your more seasoned travelers.

... you miss a week due to illness or a schedule conflict?

Make this study a top priority, but you may have to miss a week due to circumstances beyond your control. Have an assistant leader in place from the outset. It's also a great idea to let them lead part of the time while you're present.

... the group doesn't want to stop at the end of the study?

What a wonderful outcome! Discuss and agree upon the logistics of continuing to meet: curriculum, location, accountability, etc. Don't pressure people into staying or make them feel guilty if they choose not to.

Here are some additional questions you can use to stimulate discussion on key points brought up in the book and the film but not covered in the earlier in this study guide.

Supplementa

Supplemental Questions

❓ WK1

These questions are based on Act I of the film *Grow Together: A Conversation Starter Film* and chapters 1 - 3 of the book *Grow Together*.

Researcher Ed Stetzer found that of those who regularly attended youth group as teens, only about 30 percent continue regular church attendance as 20-somethings. A lower percentage of Millennials attend church than any previous generation in American history. Today the rising generation is called the "Nones," as in, "What is your religious preference?" "None."

FAKE!

❝ When I talk to young people who are leaving the church, the number one thing I hear is that it's fake. It's fake. And young people can see right through the façade. I don't blame them. I wouldn't sign up for something that's fake either."
—Pete Briscoe

Why do you think the church is seen as fake and inauthentic?

What has to be happening on a consistent basis within the church for it to be a transformational community?

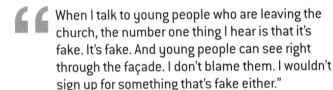

TOO ORGANIZED?

> Being organized is important. And organizing people by dividing them by age groups is such a common thing today that we rarely stop to ask whether it's a good idea, or whether it actually works. Youth program here, college program over there, singles gather up! Don't like the music? Don't fight about it. Just separate. Do your own thing. No big deal."

Organizing people by age groups is now so common that we rarely stop to ask whether it's a good idea or whether it actually works. As with society in general, people are pigeonholed from cradle to grave.

What are some of the advantages of being grouped with our peers?

What are some of the drawbacks of being separated from other age groups?

Generational silos can erode the authenticity of the church community and hinder the passing of the faith from one generation to the next. **In your opinion, which church programs should be age-divided and which should be multigenerational?**

WK2

These questions are based on Act II of the film *Grow Together: A Conversation Starter Film* and chapters 4 - 6 of the book *Grow Together*.

THE GREAT DIVIDE

" Nothing divides the generations quite like technology. Most older adults speak technology with an accent that says to the next generation, "You're not from here, are you?" That can't help but disrupt communication.

Technology itself isn't bad; it just accents the differences that already exist. Different ways of communicating and handling information spill over into every area of life, including the church."

Can you give some examples of how the generations differ when it comes to technology?

What natural tensions exist between the technically literate and technically illiterate?

Look around on Sunday morning and see how many people are holding Bibles and how many are looking at iPads. By the way, which one is the preacher using?

How has technology helped the church?

How has it done damage?

What are some ways the timeless message of the church can be communicated with timely methods?

Refusing to go to church and forsaking a biblical worldview are symptoms of a larger disease: purposelessness. Four out of five young people ages 12 to 22 say they don't know where they are going in life and why they would go there in the first place. This is not a generation that is temporarily disoriented on the way to its destination; it has no destination.

A SENSE OF PURPOSE

 All people hunger for an answer to the question, "Who am I?" We desperately want to believe what Pulitzer Prize winning novelist Frederick Buechner says, "The place God calls you to is the place where your deep gladness and the world's deep hunger meet." But we wonder: What does this place look like and how might we get there? How can we satisfy the world's hunger if we can't even satisfy our own?"

Amidst the chaos of everyday life, do you have a clear sense of purpose? Some idea of who you are and where you're going? How would you complete this sentence,

I exist to ...

Take some time to ponder this. Ask your spouse, family and friends what they think and see if you can come up with a completed sentence. Once you have a Life Sentence, share it with the group or other close friends. See if they think it describes you.

❓ WK3

These questions are based on Act III of the film *Grow Together: A Conversation Starter Film* and chapters 7 and 8 of the book *Grow Together*.

We need a new metaphor. One that reflects an actual change of heart, that recognizes that dysfunctional processes are not fixed by making them faster or more efficient. How about the idea of "cultivating"? To cultivate means to nurture, foster; to seek the goodwill of; to improve, tend; to promote the growth of; to form, refine; to prepare to bear fruit.

NEW METAPHOR

We have to release our manufacturing metaphor, release the idea that we can shape people in the same way that we make toasters, by standardizing our processes and mass-producing them. To manufacture means to make by manual labor, fabricate; to produce mechanically; to work up into form for use; to reproduce without inspiration or originality.

With cultivating, there are so many variables: weather, soil conditions, acts of nature. The final outcome is out of our hands. But isn't that the way it is with relationships? All true influence involves tending, not assembling; nurturing, not engineering.

Can you give some examples of how the generations differ when it comes to technology?

Are the programs and body life in your church more reminiscent of cultivating or manufacturing?

How can the church do more cultivating and less manufacturing? More influencing and less controlling?

When it comes to sharing Christ with the world, are we manufacturing, or are we cultivating?

BOSS OR BUDDY

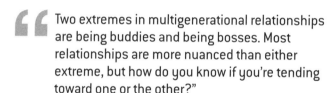 Two extremes in multigenerational relationships are being buddies and being bosses. Most relationships are more nuanced than either extreme, but how do you know if you're tending toward one or the other?"

What are some characteristics of being bossy?

What are some characteristics of being buddies?

❓ WK4

These questions are based on Act III of the film *Grow Together: A Conversation Starter Film* and chapters 9 and 10 of the book *Grow Together*.

GOOD SHEPHERDS

In addition to metaphors about cultivation and growth, the metaphor of "shepherd" in scripture describes a uniquely biblical kind of leadership. It occurs more than a hundred times and serves as an apt description for the kind of leader who creates a safe place for people to satisfy their hunger for truth, identity and meaning.

What are some of the characteristics of a good shepherd? (Feel free to consult Psalm 23 and other relevant biblical passages.)

How important is it that shepherds make those who are following them feel safe?

How will followers respond if they feel unsafe?

The first response of many people when the subject of mentoring comes up is to say, "I can't do this."

RELUCTANT MENTORS

 The potential mentors say, "I don't have what it takes, I'm not wise enough, I don't have the time, I have nothing to give." And the mentees are saying, "Nobody wants to spend time with me, and I don't even know if I need that, and maybe I'm fine by myself." –Esther Fleece

Mentoring isn't for professionals; it's for learners who are willing to share the learning process with others. Can you think of some reasons why being seen as an "expert" could actually be a determent to mentoring?

If you are older, what keeps you from being a mentor?

If you are younger, what keeps you from being a mentee?

Notes

MORE FOOD FOR THOUGHT

Here are additional quotes from *Grow Together* that highlight some of Dr. Myers' key points. Meditate on these as you prepare for group discussion.

CHAPTER 1

History is a river, drawing together great happenings with the small ones, swirling their individual molecules together until their separate actions blend into the flow. What we do as individuals is both irrelevant in the larger sweep of things and at the same time irreplaceable. History moves ceaselessly within time's unyielding banks and we are both being carried along and altering its course through the tens of thousands of decisions and choices we make every day.

The threat is real, but this is not a book of doom. We may yet change course and flourish. But whether we do so is not a decision of individual wills. We must together decide to change because at the center of our choosing is not a solitary soul but a body — an institution given by God. It's called the church.

To people with a small view of church, such a claim is absurd. A large part of the problem is thinking of church as a place we go or a duty we fulfill rather than what it really is: an extraordinary idea about a way to connect with others that transforms human relationships and leads to an extraordinary transformation of society.

CHAPTER 2

Win Arn, founder of Church Growth, Inc., claims that out of the 350,000 churches in America, four out of five have plateaued or are declining. Around 3,500 to 4,000 churches close their doors every year, he calculates. With more than 200 million non-church-goers, America now ranks in the top four least-churched nations in the world.

Metaphors matter. For example, thinking of people as machines leads us to wrongly conceive of humanity as that which can be programmed, controlled, tinkered with, organized and, as the definition of manufacturing states, produced "mechanically without inspiration or originality."

The deepest and most enduring metaphors for humanity, those that represent what is truly better, are of the earth. They are nuanced and humble, yet gracefully powerful. Fruitfulness rather than productivity. Cultivation rather than manufacturing. Abundance rather than stockpiling. Seeds rather than parts.

CHAPTER 3

Most worldviews are either materialist, believing only in the physical world, or immaterialist, believing the physical world is an illusion. Materialists have no logical reason for caring about anything "soulish" such as humans having inherent spiritual value. Immaterialists have no logical reason to care about improving things in this illusory world.

The Christian worldview transcends other worldviews' self-imposed boundaries, revealing instead an immaterial and transcendent God who, as Father, Son and Holy Spirit, exists in an eternal relationship within himself. This God, in turn, created the material world and made human beings, not as slaves but as divinely equipped, breathed-into, bearers of the Imago Dei.

Failure to pass on godly principles in one generation always leads to bloodshed in the next, whether at the hands of a tyrant like Hitler, who condemned those he wished were never born, or through the pens of Supreme Court justices whose signatures ensure that they never will be. Where many men are soft, a few hard men will rule.

CHAPTER 4

More and more people are starting to grasp that Christianity approaches the question of truth as a comprehensive worldview, a set of ideas, patterns, values and behaviors that encompass everything in the world. Just as Jesus instructed his disciples to teach people to obey God in every area of life because "all authority in heaven and on earth" belongs to him (Matthew 28:18-20), we are to form, fill, create and restore, all in the authority of Christ.

But only half of today's pastors express confidence in the truth of basic Christian doctrines such as the accuracy of the Bible, Jesus' sinless nature, salvation by grace alone and the omnipotence of God. Untethered from these doctrines, Christianity stands silent in the presence of life's ultimate questions. And pastoral uncertainties filter down; less than 10 percent of born-again Christians actually possess a Christian worldview.

Righteous living in one's own lifetime is not enough. ... There is no righteousness that does not include investing in future generations. And people who have figured this out have literally changed the world.

CHAPTER 5

It's a question of identity. Most people define their identity in terms of success: income, possessions and reputation. But at a deeper level, as bearers of the Imago Dei, we find ourselves tempted by two idols that poison our thinking, leaving us lost and confused. The first idol is persona. Today's online world makes it possible — easy, really — to transcend our circumstances and project an image of our hoped-for selves. Is this projection an illusion or reality? Do we even know, and would we admit it if we did?

Second, we are tempted by the idol of tribe, wrapping our identities around hobbies, musical taste, athletic ability or some other cultural preference we share with those we approve of or whose approval we hope to win. As a consequence, we root ourselves in that which cannot last while uprooting that which can.

Questions are the key. It's how Jesus did it. Paul Stanley points out: "Jesus asked 288 questions in the gospels. He already knew the answers to all of these questions, but he asked them anyway. It just shows how important questions are in the relationship to spark thinking, involvement and responsibility."

CHAPTER 6

In all the universe, the church is the natural home to what is robust, fruitful, victorious and full of ultimate meaning. Not just in a church, as in a particular church building, but in the universal church, the body of Christ, a group of losers for whom perfection is a far-off dream and who flail, toddler-like, steadied by God's ever-patient hand, until at last we grow up and become a beautiful bride. Not individually, mind you. Together.

Sociologist Peter Berger has noted that being together with other believers is one of the key factors that makes a serious faith plausible: "To have a conversion experience is nothing much. The real thing is to be able to keep taking it seriously; to retain a sense of its plausibility. This is where the religious community comes in."

The only way to show rising generations that church is something you are, not something to go to, is to make it personal. It's like a birthday party, not a drive-through. A wedding reception, not a concert. A family reunion, not an amusement park. But knowing this in theory does us little good. If what we've learned so far in this book is true, our own hunger for truth, identity and meaning will be satisfied only as we meet others' hunger.

CHAPTER 7

Life-on-life relationships have changed the world and saved civilization. It's the church's true secret. But what stops us from achieving this radical transformation is, more than anything, a simple failure to turn the minutes of life into moments of eternal significance.

God's message is clear: It is through relationships in the context of the body of Christ that people's hunger for truth, for identity and for meaning are satiated. People are hungry and you are the one with the groceries. Let joy replace fear and start cooking. It will be beautiful. … God doesn't ask us to steward resources we don't possess, but he does ask us to get our priorities straight. Lynn Harold Houg says, "The tragedy of the world is that men have given first-class loyalty to second-class causes, and these causes have betrayed them."

CHAPTER 8

In many churches, it is assumed that teaching occurs when a pastor preaches or a Sunday school teacher gives a lecture. This isn't the main way Jesus taught, though. He occasionally addressed the crowds, but mostly he walked and talked, discussed, asked and answered questions, told stories, engaged in debates, and used outdoor activities to get his point across. It is said that a good teacher is like a candle, consuming itself to light the way for others. Teacher and author Parker Palmer says that all good teachers have a capacity for connectedness: "Good teachers weave a fabric of connectedness … and the loom on which they do the weaving is their own heart."

Often churches, in pursuit of efficiency and measurable growth, try to hype members into joining accountability groups to acknowledge sin, Bible reading programs to enhance Bible literacy, or growth groups that focus on improving outward behavior. Unfortunately, as good as these outcomes are, they can miss what God is really after — not well-behaved moralists but people who love him with all of their hearts, souls and minds.

CHAPTER 9

Psalm 23 talks about God as a shepherd who is both with the sheep and guiding them. In his book *Mentoring for Mission*, Gunter Krallmann calls this let's-walk-together approach "transparent with-ness." Transparent with-ness transcends idiocy (idios is the Greek word for what we alone know) and blossoms in koinonia, or knowing community.

Transparent with-ness puts a premium on safety, not so people can be complacent but to enable them to take greater risks. Safety is to leadership growth what a net is to a trapeze artist. People are freer to accept the challenge of real growth when they feel safe in the company of those leading them.

No matter their generation, when people are approached from the standpoint of understanding, they usually respond with a strong desire to form relationships. Even the toughest young person longs to connect with a caring adult. Multigenerational relationships not only help satisfy people's craving for truth, identity and meaning … they also strengthen the church to rise to the occasion when opportunities — or even terrifying events — arise.

CHAPTER 10

As a youth, a mentor asked me, "What do you have that is so worth living for that you'd be willing to die for it?" The question startled me. I knew right then that I would choose to live intentionally. That experience began a process of change in my life. Three decades later I faced a critical moment that challenged this commitment to the core. It was 1:30 in the morning, and through my window I could see flames atop the ridge from the Waldo Canyon wildfire spreading quickly in our direction, threatening to destroy our town of Manitou Springs.

Our last-minute evacuation plan called for us to evacuate our 180 students, 40 summer staff and around 30 full-time staff and their families to Mountain Springs Church. Some churches might dread such an invasion, but Mountain Springs' security guy, Rob, was all for it. "We want you here," he said. It's one thing to be taken in during an emergency. It's another thing altogether to have them want you to come.

When it came to supplies, Mountain Springs' pastor Steve told me, "Don't worry. We sent out a notice on Twitter. We'll get all the supplies we need." I looked at my watch. Who on earth is checking their Twitter feed at 2:30 in the morning? Apparently, a lot of people. Within minutes a parade of headlights appeared, minivans and pickups dropping off sleeping bags and cases of bottled water. Over the next 24 hours Mountain Springs members brought piles and piles of supplies: food, toothpaste, shampoo, pillows, towels. Those who couldn't bring supplies brought money. Exceeding, abundant provision.

Across Colorado Springs churches stepped up to serve the more than 32,000 evacuees. For one week there were no denominations. And no generations. Young and old worked side by side, called together by an urgent cause. Imagine the church similarly facing down the cultural challenges of our age. We are one body that includes every tribe and tongue. And generation. This is our opportunity. Decades hence, people will look back at our age, with all of its potential, and ask whether we stewarded it well.

If you aren't currently involved in mentoring, take advantage of the natural opportunities that already exist in your church:

ENGAGE!

ENGAGE!

✝ EXISTING OPPORTUNITIES

Find out what opportunities your church offers for life-on-life interaction and get involved. Don't be afraid to experiment. Try different ministries until you find something that fits. Learn from the more experienced. Teach the less experienced. Do your part.

SUNDAY SCHOOL AND CHILDREN'S MINISTRIES

Sunday school is the time when the average layperson is most likely to get involved with the younger generation. The structure is already in place and it's easy to plug in for a short-term or long-term commitment. Consider volunteering to teach or help in a classroom.

YOUTH MINISTRY

This represents perhaps the greatest opportunity to engage the emerging generation in life-on-life mentoring. Many teenagers want more personal interaction with adult role models. Why not provide a host home for a few activities or act as a driver or chaperone for some events to get your feet wet?

FAMILY MINISTRY

You are most likely to give your greatest emotional and physical energy to areas where your own family is concerned. Equipping parents to mentor, and find mentors for their own children, will strengthen the whole body, so look for opportunities to interact informally or in more structured programs with other families.

MEN'S AND WOMEN'S MINISTRIES

Everyone is a potential mentor or mentoree since you can look to someone who is further along the path of life than you are as well as see others who are coming behind you. Find ways to connect with role models you respect, and be open to being a role model yourself. Prayer or accountability groups, Bible studies or service groups are good places to start.

OUTREACH MINISTRIES

Life-on-life mentoring isn't bound by church walls. It should be incorporated into all forms of outreach into your neighborhood, city and world. Veteran leaders should recruit and train people who have a heart for ministry and want to test the waters. An apprenticeship model works best; it's the way Jesus trained his disciples.

> " Instead, speaking the truth in love, we will in all things grow up into him who is the Head, that is, Christ. From him the whole body, joined and held together by every supporting ligament, grows and builds itself up in love, *as each part does its work.*"
> —Ephesians 4:15-16

ⓔ EXAMPLES

These churches serve as good examples of how to cultivate life-on-life relationships.

COACHING IN THE CHURCH

The word "coach" often refers to an athletic instructor, a mentor or even a New Age guru teaching people to channel their inner power. At root, though, a coach is one who leads another by walking alongside and helping that person maintain forward motion.

Coach trainer Tony Stoltzfus, among many others, has moved coaching from the workplace to the church. He's found that regardless of the area of life, people perform better when others believe in them and express confidence that God is working in them, that they can solve their own problems and that their coach is on their side.

At **Hill Country Bible Church Northwest** in Austin, Texas, church leaders have embraced mentor/coaching to the point of taking their leadership through coach training workshops. According to Annette Boorman, generations team leader at Hill Country, church leaders now use coaching questions to help people set goals for spiritual growth. Annette explains: "Our philosophy of ministry comes out in the three questions we ask: 'Who are you?' 'Where are you spiritually?' and 'How can I help you take your next step?'"

Before these questions will be taken seriously, Hill Country members have to know and genuinely care about people. That's where coaching comes in. Hill Country equips their congregation with basic coaching skills so they can connect with others across generations on a more meaningful level.

Recognizing that parents often have a difficult time conversing with their own children, Annette's team uses coach training to help parents talk with their kids. Even if they begin with goofy questions like, 'If you could only eat one thing for the rest of your life, what would it be and why?' Annette says, it begins a dialogue that is the foundation for spiritual growth. Hill Country also sets aside time in their children's Sunday school classes for parents to come into the classroom to coach their own children.

Does your church provide ongoing training to equip people to be more effective leaders? More effective mentors? More effective parents?

If this area needs developing or strengthening, can you help start a pilot training program?

Are you aware of coaching resources your church could take advantage of? Seminars, books, online resources, consultants?

Why not introduce your church leadership to resources you or those you know have found beneficial?

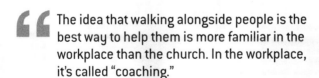

The idea that walking alongside people is the best way to help them is more familiar in the workplace than the church. In the workplace, it's called "coaching."

(e) EXAMPLES

PARADIGM SHIFT

It took a near tragedy for **Calvary Community Church** in Westlake Village, California, to connect the generations in a way that satisfies our hunger for meaning. Drew Sams, pastor of student ministries, shares the story: "For years we had tried to make students 'busy for Jesus' by providing exciting events and programs that they would want to do."

Drew's youth group was thriving, but everything came to a screeching halt when one of their top students — a young man who was involved in leadership, small group and missions — attempted suicide. Shocked, Drew and his team realized they had labeled this student a "success" while knowing nothing of his struggles.

Something wasn't right about this picture. How could one of their seemingly best-known students — who was so often in the spotlight — have been dealing with such deep pain without any of the adult leaders knowing anything about it?

That's when it hit them: No other spotlight in the world can illuminate the heart the way a personal relationship can. With that realization came a paradigm shift; what their youth ministry needed was to shift its focus from numbers, events and a full calendar of ministry activities to life-on-life involvement with their students.

Drew describes how this paradigm shift has played out: "One of the many practical ways we have [brought about this shift] is through equipping volunteers, parents and students to be present in each other's lives. Our events calendar is emptier than it used to be, but now we are free to go to students, listen and care unconditionally for them."

Rather than focusing on programs, Drew and his staff have realized that the most important thing they can do in their youth ministry is to cultivate life-on-life relationships with their students.

The only way to show rising generations that church is something you are, not something to go to, is to make it personal. It's like a birthday party, not a drive-through. A wedding reception, not a concert. A family reunion, not an amusement park.

Does your church have a good balance between programs and opportunities to develop life-on-life relationships?

If you think programs and relational time are out of balance, what would be some helpful corrections?

How's the balance in your own life between church activities and spending time building and enjoying relationships?

Are there church activities you do out of a sense of guilt or concern about what others will think if you don't attend? If so, give yourself permission to "drop out" so you can "plug in."

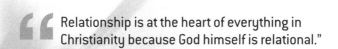

Relationship is at the heart of everything in Christianity because God himself is relational."

ⓔ EXAMPLES

AMATEURS WELCOME

Helping another person discover purpose and identity is a matter of cultivating, not manufacturing. You don't have to be a professional. Keith Anderson and Randy Reese explain:

> *God's heart has already felt and loved and hoped before we ever arrived. The songs of our soul have already been whispered and sung into our souls. If this notion is true, and we believe passionately that it is, then the work of the mentor is not to create but to notice, not to invent but to discern.*

The message is this: "God is working in both of our lives. I see what God is doing in your life and I want to be part of the process of him shaping you into who he wants you to be."

You don't need to be a professional to mentor. In fact, that could get in the way. In 2003, **Watermark Community Church** in Dallas was a small group of believers meeting in a warehouse. One of those believers, Bill Roberson, joined with another like-minded man to start a small group Bible study.

"Most of these people had never had any life-on-life discipleship in their Christian walk," Bill recalls. "Most of us were just dropped at the church doorstep to figure it out on our own." Soon there were 400 people in these groups being discipled by 60 leaders, and Watermark itself had grown to upward of 5,000 congregants.

The church doesn't staff this effort. There is no budget. And yet so many congregants are involved in this grassroots movement that life-on-life discipleship has become the norm church-wide.

Are you participating in any informal groups or ministries in which life-on-life mentoring is occurring?

If you are, can you think of others you could invite to join you?

If you aren't, are there opportunities you should consider?

Not all ministry takes place from the top down. A healthy church is one where the whole body is involved in "building itself up in love, as each part does its work (Ephesians 4:16).

In terms of participation, how would you rate the body life in your church?

Are you involved in ministry at your church, either internally or as part of an outreach?

If you're over-committed, where do you need to cut back?

If you're under-involved, where can you plug in?

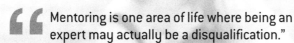

Mentoring is one area of life where being an expert may actually be a disqualification."

e EXAMPLES

NEVER TOO OLD

Marilyn Jarrett's nimble fingers deftly work a needle, bringing cloth to life in colorful threads as she carefully follows an intricate pattern. Embroidery is a passion of Marilyn's, but she has an even greater passion for seeing God's faithful hand reproducing the image of His Son in the lives of others through discipleship.

Retired schoolteacher Marilyn, 82, and a growing number of men and women at **Zionsville Presbyterian Church** in the Indianapolis suburb, see one-to-one mentoring as a gift, not a task.

Marilyn has been mentoring Jill Tanner, a 48-year-old mother in her church, for about a year and a half. Every two weeks, Jill drives down a country road to spend an hour or more at Marilyn's house. Beyond reading the materials together, their conversation inevitably moves toward events in Jill's life. Marilyn listens intently to Jill. Her guidance is both gentle and firm, blending the voices of friend and mother.

Relatively few Christians today enjoy the God-given gift of this kind of relationship, says Marilyn's friend Donna Bahler. The basic element is often there — friendship and a mutual faith in Jesus. But the more complicated parts of discipleship — being intentional and following a transferrable pattern — are something Marilyn has learned from Donna, a Cru staff member.

Donna modeled discipleship for Marilyn and a few other women at ZPC. "For them, discipleship had come through so many channels over such a period of time," says Donna, "that it was hard to put it together into a way that they could turn around and use with someone else."

Since then, 125 women at ZPC have learned the discipleship process, with the strong support of Marilyn's pastor, Glenn McDonald. Author of *The Disciple-Making Church*, Pastor Glenn sees the importance of corporate worship and one-to-one discipleship in the development of the believer.

Since 1998, Marilyn has been intentional in her time with one or two women at a time, and she knows they too will be able to mentor other women, as several of them have already begun doing. Marilyn lives out 2 Timothy 2:2, entrusting the things she's learned to reliable women who will teach others.

Marilyn speaks from experience: "Anybody who wants to mentor can mentor. We all have something we can pass on to someone else." And as Marilyn has found, being a mentor is as much of a blessing to her as it is to the women she mentors. "I get as much out of it as they do," she admits. It is a gift she refuses to pass up.

Excerpted from the article by Hayley Newsom on Cru.org,
http://www.cru.org/training-and-growth/mentoring/to-learn-twice-marilyn-jarrett.htm

Have you ever felt too old or unqualified to be a mentor?
Don't sell yourself short. Remember that the longer you've lived, the more you've learned that you can pass on to the younger generation.

What are some of the natural relationships you have that could be turned into mentoring relationships, with you as either the mentor or the mentee? Why not raise at least one relationship to the mentoring level?

Does your church have a discipleship or mentor-training program? If it does — and you haven't taken it — consider signing up.

If your church doesn't have a program, or if you would like additional training, ask your pastor or other leaders you respect for recommendations. There are many excellent programs available online or offered by ministries in your area.

 Strong social bonds depend on the ability to understand and respond empathetically to others' experiences."

ABOUT SUMMIT MINISTRIES

An alarming number of Christians stumble while in college, and around half will renounce their faith because they simply do not have a defense for what they believe. David Noebel founded Summit in 1962 to help ground Christians in their faith, enabling them to face the challenges that a post-Christian culture presents to followers of Jesus.

Summit equips Christians to think faithfully and engage courageously through conferences, curricula and content.

Conferences. Each of Summit's one-of-kind conference settings creates mentoring communities in which expert instructors equip students to fearlessly embrace and defend truth. Summit's renowned two-week programs for 16- to 21-year-old students take place every summer in Colorado and across the U.S.

Summit also offers Institutes — longer study programs with collegiate credits. Summit Semester serves as a gap-year program for students headed to top universities. Summit Oxford is a study-abroad program in which invited students study in one of three exclusive colleges of Oxford University. In each of these Institutes, students receive advanced worldview training and mentoring.

Curricula. With the goal of solid biblical thinking and cultural engagement, Summit has become a leading-edge provider of accessible, biblically faithful and academically credible curricula for Christian schools, homeschools and churches. Our seminal work *Understanding the Times* is one of the best-selling worldview textbooks of all time.

Content. Today, with its world-renowned faculty and under the direction of President Dr. Jeff Myers, Summit is viewed as one of the foremost leaders in training Christians to think faithfully and engage culture. Summit aims to provide a thorough grasp of the biblical, Christian worldview and prepare believers to analyze today's competing worldviews in the light of Truth. Summit provides a number of helpful resources including books, videos, a monthly Journal, original articles, streaming lectures and more.

Learn more at summit.org